Original title:
Melon Whispers

Copyright © 2025 Creative Arts Management OÜ
All rights reserved.

Author: Natalia Harrington
ISBN HARDBACK: 978-1-80586-403-5
ISBN PAPERBACK: 978-1-80586-875-0

Drenched in Honeyed Sighs

Under the sun, they giggle and roll,
Sticky fingers, a sweetened stroll.
Nature's candy, bursting with cheer,
Each nibble met with a joyful tear.

Bouncing laughter, they chase in the field,
Fruit-filled secrets, hilarity revealed.
Unexpected splashes, a juicy surprise,
Who knew fruit could cause such sly lies?

Juicy Reverie Under Starlit Skies

Party hats made of vine and zest,
Under the stars, we eat with the best.
Laughter echoes, we face the night,
With slices so sweet, everything's right.

Fruits on sticks, our silly design,
A tasty mess, always divine.
Spitting seeds like confetti in air,
We dance 'neath the moon, without a care.

Tales Woven in Verdant Vines

A tale of fruit, so curious and bold,
Giggles grow from stories retold.
Each playful twist, a chuckle so vast,
Woven with joy from summers passed.

Tendrils of laughter snake through the grass,
Tasting the rewards as good memories amass.
Grapes trampoline, bouncing so high,
While whispered secrets float up to the sky.

The Lure of the Harvest Moon

When the moon rises, we gather with glee,
A circus of fruits, oh what a sight to see!
With goofy grins, we dive for the prize,
Remembering the joy underneath starry skies.

The harvest calls, with whispers of fun,
A merry adventure for everyone.
Laughter flavors the night like fine wine,
As we celebrate life, so brightly we shine.

Enchanted by Nature's Bounty

In a patch of green, a fruit so round,
Laughter echoes, a joy profound.
A splash of juice, a sticky grin,
Who knew such bliss could come from skin?

Bouncing on vines like children at play,
Sunshine giggles at the end of the day.
Tickling toes in the grass so soft,
Nature's delight makes our spirits loft.

Echoes of the Orchard's Heart

Under trees tall, with branches wide,
Fruits laugh together, side by side.
A tickle of breeze, a fruity affair,
Their whispers charm without a care.

A rolling laugh as treasures roll,
Sweetness drips, it's good for the soul.
Orchard's dance in the golden light,
Jubilant fruits, a merry sight.

Harvesting Dreams Under the Sun

With baskets round, we sing a tune,
Gathering joy in the warm afternoon.
Silly grapes join the high-flying fun,
Wobble and tumble, oh what a run!

Chasing shadows, we laugh and spin,
Plucking dreams from where laughter's been.
A carnival feast awaits on the ground,
Bouncing flavors, everywhere found!

Whiffs of Hidden Delicacies

In the garden's realm, surprises hide,
A whiff of magic from the vine's side.
Nose in the air, what delights prevail,
A fruity whisper ticks off the scale!

Lemonade laughter spurts from the tree,
Ticklish flavors, oh, what glee!
Giggles and grins with every bite,
Where every snack feels just right!

Golden Days and Glistening Nights

In fields so bright, where laughter rolls,
A fruit of joy fills happy souls.
With every slice, the sweetness gleams,
Bursting forth like summer dreams.

The sun dips low, the shades grow long,
We dance to nature's zesty song.
Little bites, a chuckle shared,
In juicy bites, our hearts laid bare.

The Quiet Lullaby of Flesh and Seed

In gardens lush, a secret told,
A belly full, we laugh so bold.
The seeds inside begin to roam,
As whispers carry us back home.

With each crunch, a giggle flies,
A fruit that makes us touch the skies.
A serenade of flavor sweet,
In harmony, our laughter meets.

Beneath the Veil of Green

Beneath leaves thick, a treasure hides,
With playful glee, the fun abides.
Surprise! A slice, so chilled and bright,
A tasty prank of sheer delight.

We scoop and share, a joyful mess,
With every seed, we laugh, confess.
In summer's glow, our joy expands,
As fruit-filled magic fills our hands.

The Taste of Harmony and Light

A party planned with friends so dear,
We toast with juice, spread summer cheer.
The colors dance and flavors mix,
In playful bites, we find our fix.

The sweetness tickles, laughter rolls,
In fruit's embrace, we lose our roles.
With every laugh, the joy ignites,
A feast of bliss through days and nights.

Nature's Gentle Invitations

In the garden where laughter spills,
Tiny creatures dance on hills.
The soil tickles roots below,
As sunshine tickles seeds to grow.

Raindrops fall like playful jests,
Sprouting dreams from nature's quests.
With each breeze, a giggle flies,
Inviting joy beneath the skies.

Bursting with Life's Embrace

Jolly fruits in shades of cheer,
Popping colors, bright and clear.
Bouncing berries matching beats,
In a world of delicious treats.

Joyful petals wave in glee,
Nature's laughter, wild and free.
Laughter echoes through the vines,
As sweetness drips, and sunshine shines.

The Palette of Nature's Delight

Crayons in the fields delight,
Painting blooms in colors bright.
Pinks and yellows, quite the sight,
Nature's canvas, pure and light.

Brushstrokes dance on gentle breeze,
Swirling laughter through the trees.
Each petal sings a merry song,
In this land where all belong.

Tidal Waves of Summer's Essence

Waves of warmth both bright and bold,
Tickling toes, a tale retold.
Sandy castles rise to cheer,
As giggles wash away each fear.

Splashing puddles, sunny spark,
Makes each heart a little lark.
With every wave, a happy dream,
Riding high on summer's beam.

Cradled in Nature's Embrace

In the field, fruit giggles loud,
Underneath the sun, they feel so proud.
Bouncing in the breeze, they sway with glee,
Whispers of sweetness, come dance with me!

A bite brings chuckles, a squirt of juice,
It's a juicy prank, no need to seduce.
Seeds go flying, a party in hand,
Nature's jesters, oh, isn't it grand?

In each cheery crunch, laughter cascades,
Filling up the air, like playful charades.
Freshness abounds in this rustic place,
Nature's embrace is a sweet, warm embrace!

The Hidden Symphony of Flavor

A fruity parade on a sunny day,
Taste buds doing the cha-cha, hooray!
With every nibble, a tune comes alive,
Nature's orchestra, oh how they thrive!

The red ones wink, the green ones grin,
All play together, let the feast begin!
Their juicy laughter sings a sweet song,
Creating a medley where all belong.

A sprinkle of salt, a dash of humor,
Each bite a giggle, becoming a rumor.
In every fiber, a joke lingers near,
A mischievous burst, so dear to hear!

Savoring Summer's Sweetest Moments

Under the sun, sweet secrets unfold,
A splash of delight, both silly and bold.
Laughter erupts with a playful bite,
Every slice tastes like pure delight!

Juicy dribbles become summer stains,
Wiping them off, we're laughing like planes.
Oh, sticky fingers and giggles galore,
In every morsel, we all want more!

The clock slows down as flavors unite,
Every moment is tasty, what a sight!
With tongues outstretched for the next sweet round,
In summer's laughter, joy can be found!

Sun-Touched Memories and Soft Cries

Golden rays peel back the day's bright skin,
Fruity mishaps spark laughter within.
A splash of juice, a giggle escapes,
Summer's laughter in funny shapes!

Each bite a memory, too sweet to resist,
Elixir of childhood, sprinkled with mist.
Loving the chaos, we dive into joy,
What's better than eating? Oh, the ploy!

So here's to the spills, the joy, and the mess,
In every soft cry, there's fun to express.
In sunshine and sweetness, we'll play and cheer,
These moments of laughter, we hold so dear!

The Hidden Nectar of Life's Feast

In the garden where laughter blooms,
Fruits giggle in their cozy rooms.
A slice of joy with every bite,
Sticky fingers, a sweet delight.

Seeds of gossip bounce around,
With every crunch, new tales abound.
Juicy secrets dribble down,
As we feast without a frown.

Mellow Notes of the Orchard

Underneath the sun's warm glow,
Chubby fruits swing to and fro.
They wear their rinds like silly hats,
Sharing jokes with the passing rats.

The breeze hums a tune so sweet,
While birds dance on their tiny feet.
Laughter ripples through the trees,
As nature giggles in the breeze.

Symphony of Ripeness and Sun

In a world of colors so intense,
Fruits gather for a fun suspense.
They sing in chorus, round and bright,
Creating joy from day to night.

Cherries chuckle with a pop,
As pineapples start to hop.
The sun sets low, they all unite,
In a dance of sweetness, pure delight.

A Tapestry of Earthly Delights

Beneath the vines, a treasure's found,
Funny faces all around.
With every slice, a giggle grows,
Nature's joke, the world bestows.

Round and plump, they can't hide,
Their inner jokes, they won't abide.
As we share in the fruity cheer,
Life is tasty, that much is clear.

Golden Whispers of the Garden

In the garden of giggles, fruits wear a grin,
Plump and round, they invite all kin.
A peach winks slyly, a pear does a dance,
While cucumbers chuckle at the strange romance.

The tomatoes are blushing, it's quite a sight,
As carrots tell secrets in the soft moonlight.
Each berry bursts forth with a giggly cheer,
While veggies gossip in the sunny sphere.

Bees buzz with laughter around the bright blooms,
As radishes plot in their secret rooms.
The sweet scents of joy fill the bright, warm air,
In this quirky garden, you'll find silly fare.

So come grab a snack, hear the fruit's jokes too,
With every bite, taste the laughter anew.
In this merry patch, silliness grows wide,
Join in the fun, let your worries slide.

The Allure of Nature's Sweetness

Beneath the sun's gaze, a quirky show,
A dance of flavors, come see them glow.
The berries are plotting a juicy coup,
While apples giggle, "We've got the stew!"

A zesty lemon tries to tell a tale,
But limes roll their eyes, saying, "Not for sale!"
Peas in their pods laugh at the plight,
Of mushrooms who think they've got style and height.

In the patch of delight, the squash plays a tune,
With beats so fresh, you'll bounce like a balloon.
The cucumbers boast of their cool, crisp flair,
As peppers tell tales of fiery despair.

So join the parade of nature's sweet cheer,
Each munch a giggle, every crunch a jeer.
In this carnival of flavor and fun,
Let laughter and sweetness unite as one.

Echoes of the Vineyard's Embrace

In the garden where shadows sing,
Laughter bounces on a spring.
Fruits giggle in the sunlit air,
Tickling toes without a care.

Vines twist like a jester's dance,
Bouncing berries take a chance.
A grape in trousers, a peach in hats,
How did they get into those spats?

Sipping sunshine in a glass,
Grapes in grapples, oh what sass!
Bottles rolling down the hill,
Making us laugh until we spill.

A toast to laughter, bright and bold,
With fruity tales, as tales unfold.
In the vineyard we find our glee,
Sipping joy, carefree as can be.

Sun-Drenched Melodies of Joy

Beneath the sky where sunshine beams,
Fruits hum along with silly dreams.
Plump and round, they jiggle about,
In a sunlit band, they twirl and shout.

Banana hats on berry heads,
Strawberries hopping on soft beds.
A watermelon falls; everyone giggles,
Splashes of laughter, dancing wiggles.

Squeezed into jokes and fruity puns,
Cackling joy like playful runs.
Juicy jokes that raise a cheer,
In the orchard's laughter, we draw near.

With every bite, a cheerful tune,
As nature laughs beneath the moon.
In fields of fun, we spin and play,
Every drop of joy brightens our day.

Whispers Beneath the Leafy Canopy

Leafy boughs in a gentle sway,
Fruits gossip in a comical play.
Pears are plotting a sovereign rule,
While grapes jest, oh so cool!

Here comes a squirrel with cheeky flair,
Stealing berries without a care.
The branches chuckle, a playful heist,
At the nutty thief's amusing feast.

Underneath the leafy shade,
Sunlight dapples in a cascade.
Every whisper, a tickle of fun,
Making friends of everyone.

Laughter echoes, crisp and bright,
In this haven, spirits take flight.
Nature's jest in a fruity dance,
Inviting all to join the prance.

The Scent of Warmth and Wonder

In the air, a fragrant quest,
Fruits in the sun feel truly blessed.
With zesty giggles and juicy cheers,
We dive into laughter, quenching fears.

A honeydew slips, rolls with grace,
Creating a merry, silly race.
Chasing sweetness down the lane,
Where every stumble brings a gain.

Pineapple hats on heads of fun,
Bursting with laughter, hearts weigh a ton.
A strawberry slips, oops, there it goes,
Rolling and tumbling in a funny repose.

The warmth of smiles, a fragrant breeze,
Tickling noses with fragrant ease.
In this wonder where giggles bloom,
We're lost in joy, dispelling gloom.

The Lush Echoes of Late Afternoon

In the garden, fruits collide,
Their laughter rolling, far and wide.
Slicing through the summer's hum,
Watermelons boast, 'Here we come!'

Beneath the vines, a dance unfolds,
With juicy tales, each story told.
Seeds spit out like little darts,
While sticky hands steal fruit-filled hearts.

Nectar's Gentle Serenade

Beneath the sun's warm, golden rays,
Sweet nectar drips in joyful bays.
The critters come for a taste so sweet,
As silly birds trip on tiny feet.

Laughter bubbles in the breeze,
As ants parade with playful tease.
A fruit bowl party, wild and loud,
With rinds like laughter, bright and proud.

A Slice of Sunlit Dreams

In the shade, the fruits convene,
Chattering softly, grasshoppers keen.
A slice here, a chunk there,
Creating sweetness in the air.

Picnic blankets, snacks galore,
Frolicking friends and tales to score.
Water splashes, giggles abound,
In this sunlit realm, joy is found.

Beneath the Rind, Stories Hide

Underneath the greenish skin,
A world of secrets waits within.
Whispers of fun in every bite,
Each mouthful a delight, pure light.

A secret plot from seeds that sprout,
Rolling on, they sing and shout.
Straw hats dance, and spoons collide,
In every slice, giggles reside.

Ripe Dreams in the Breeze

In the sun, they giggle loud,
Green and yellow, so very proud.
Rolling on grass, what a sight!
Bouncing around, pure delight.

With laughter, they squish and slide,
In summer's arms, they love to hide.
Juicy tales of frosty nights,
Whispering joy in playful lights.

Friends can't wait for the big slice,
Bright and sweet, it tastes so nice.
A feast of fun beneath the trees,
They dance and sway with every breeze.

Colorful Murmurs of Nature

Underneath the leafy shade,
Colors pop and jokes are made.
Orange giggles, and red grins shine,
Nature's palette, oh so divine.

They connive to spill their cheer,
Fruity banter that we hold dear.
Jokes about the picnic flares,
As laughter drips from all the pears.

Nature's chorus sings so sweet,
In harmony, their rhythms beat.
A riot of hues, all aglow,
Painting laughter where'er we go.

The Secret Poetry of Seeds

In the soil, stories weave,
Tiny tales that we believe.
With every sprout, a joke unfurls,
Funny whispers of leafy swirls.

Roots that stretch, with great intent,
Poking fun, they're quite content.
Silly puns beneath the ground,
In a clever silence, they're found.

Waiting for the sun's warm glow,
They tickle the earth, saying 'hello!'
With each bloom, a giggling cheer,
A bright bouquet of laughter here.

Dew-Kissed Afternoon Reveries

Dew drops dance on blades of green,
A sparkling show, a lovely scene.
Sunlight giggles in the glade,
As playful shadows start to fade.

Bees buzz jokes in busy flight,
Chasing daisies, what a sight!
Tickled by the gentle breeze,
The world sings softly, oh so pleased.

Each lazy hour, a silly grin,
With nature's tales, the fun begins.
In this moment, pure delight,
We laugh along with day and night.

The Gathering Storm of Sunlight

Beneath the sun, a party brews,
Fruit hats wobble, like silly shoes.
Seeds are plotted, laughter in the air,
Juicy promises, everywhere!

Sun-kissed cheeks begin to glow,
Tickling toes, we swish and flow.
Giggly gusts sweep through the day,
As we bounce in our fruity fray!

A wave of taste, so ripe and sweet,
We toast to summer, a tasty feat.
With every bite, the jokes just swell,
In the sun's embrace, all is well!

The storm rolls in, a juicy spree,
Nature's treats, come dance with me!
With every chuckle, seeds collide,
In glimmering fun, we all abide!

A Dance with Nature's Offering

A wobbling fruit parade is here,
Spin and giggle, shed your fear.
With every dance, the juice does fly,
Slippery moves, oh my, oh my!

Bouncing berries, a wiggly team,
In this fruity world, we gleam and scheme.
The rhymes are sweet, the steps are bold,
Nature's gifts, we joyfully behold!

Swaying leaves join in the play,
Laughing hearts go wild today.
Who knew fruit could bring such glee?
Nature's offerings, come dance with me!

A feast awaits, so bright, so round,
In this delightful whirling sound.
Crack a grin, take a big bite,
In this party of pure delight!

Whispers in the Dewy Dawn

Morning breaks with a giggling sound,
Droplets dance, scattered around.
A hush fills the air, ripe with surprise,
Nature whispers beneath sparkling skies.

Greenery shakes off its evening dew,
Fruit pom-poms cheer, they're ready for you!
With beams of sun coaxing it all,
Laughter echoes, a beckoning call.

Berried treasures, glistening bright,
In playful chaos, they burst with delight.
Every crunch and munch, a silly song,
In this fruity morning, we all belong!

As dew droplets tumble, tickling our toes,
Welcome, sweet laughter, wherever it goes.
In silly whispers, the fruit starts to sway,
Under the dawn, we dance and play!

Time Melting on Sweet Lips

Time, it seems, drips like syrupy fun,
Juicy moments, slip, slide, and run.
With every taste, seconds dissolve,
In this joyful riddle, we all evolve.

Sweetness lingers, a playful tease,
Laughter bubbles like a soft breeze.
Sipping sunshine from laughter's cup,
In silly antics, we can't get enough!

Each drip drops joy, an endless loop,
With fruity giggles, we form a troop.
Tasting time, with every cheer,
In this jammy bliss, we persevere!

So let's toast to laughter, ripe and grand,
Where time melts sweetly, hand in hand.
Under the sun, with smiles so wide,
In this sugary dance, let's forever glide!

Fragrant Memories of Sun-Drenched Days

Under the sun, so bright and bold,
Laughter dances, a story told.
With each slice, a burst of glee,
Juicy secrets shared with me.

Picnics start with a playful tease,
Sticky fingers, sweet as bees.
We toss the seeds, who will get sprouted?
Cheerful chaos, hearts unclouded.

The days stretch long like a warm embrace,
Sun-kissed faces, no need for grace.
Giggling under a striped canopy,
Colorful fruits inspire our symphony.

As sunset paints a blush so grand,
We're left with laughter, hand in hand.
Fragrant memories swirl and sway,
In this golden, sweet ballet.

A Symphony of Color and Flavor

A carnival riot of green and gold,
Every bite, a joke yet untold.
I juggle pieces with a wink,
Let's see who drops theirs, oh, what a stink!

Fruity confetti scattered wide,
Mismatched socks, we take in stride.
With sugary smiles, we relish the day,
Under the sky, we dance and play.

Beneath the tent, we share our rhymes,
Flavor fireworks in summertime.
Chewing and laughing, the fruit flies too,
Silly faces in a berry-blue hue.

A splash of sparkle on our chins,
The sweetest chaos, let the fun begin!
With every flavor, our hearts uplift,
In this tangy, giggly, fruity gift.

Songs of the Sun-Kissed Skin

Skin shimmering like the morning light,
We sing our tunes, oh what a sight!
With each sticky kiss, we feel alive,
A chorus of sweetness, we all connive.

Barefoot and bold, we race through the grass,
Each splash of juice a colorful pass.
With laughter ringing, we make a pact,
To embrace the folly, that's a fact!

Golden glows dance on our cheeks,
Nature's melody is what we seek.
Sun-kissed laughter fills the air,
Spontaneous moments, without a care.

In a world of flavor, we find our delight,
Songs of summer carry us into the night.
With every bite, we skip and twirl,
In this fruity sonnet, life's a whirl.

The Calm Before the Ripe

In the garden, still and bright,
Ripening dreams, a charming sight.
Anticipation paints the scene,
Like silly whispers, soft and keen.

Tick-tock goes the sunny clock,
We count the moments, take stock.
Patience blooms, a giggle fest,
Waiting for sweetness, oh what a quest!

The breeze carries a fruity hum,
As bees join in the playful drum.
What will we find in the day's embrace?
Nature's joke, a sweet face race!

With each passing hour, we grin with glee,
The calm before flavors, a jubilee.
As dusk approaches, we hold our breath,
What wonders await, life's little zest!

Anthems of the Orchard's Bounty

In a land where fruits do dance,
Laughter bursts, what a chance!
Juicy balls roll off the vine,
Silly creatures sip their wine.

Bumblebees hum a tune so sweet,
While the rabbits tap their feet.
A pig in shades, how absurd!
Dancing underneath a bird.

Giggles rise in the warm, bright sun,
Fruits unite; it's time for fun!
The fruit parade is quite a sight,
Bright colors flashing, pure delight!

Tasting games, who can resist?
Wobbling fun in a fruity mist!
Pies and smiles fill the air,
Orchard life is beyond compare!

The Glimpse of Golden Slices

Golden hues beneath the trees,
Tickling toes in the summer breeze.
Slices that grin from ear to ear,
Always coaxing hearty cheer.

Happiness spills from every core,
As laughter bounces off the floor.
Fruits sit splashed in rays of light,
Jokes exchanged in pure delight.

Boys and girls in a friendly race,
To see who can devour with grace.
Juicy bites, a sticky mess,
Fruit-filled faces, nothing less!

Pies created with silly flair,
Splat! A slice flies through the air.
Giggles echo in sunlit spaces,
Life is sweet with fruity embraces!

Juicy Secrets of the Orchard

Secrets hide in leafy groves,
Where silly critters twist and doze.
Whispers shared by ripened fruits,
Chasing critters in bright green boots.

Lemon laughs in a tangy tune,
While cherries wink at the afternoon.
"Who's juicier?" a grape will tease,
Bouncing round like they own the breeze!

Raspberry folly, a berry brawl,
Strawberries giggle, they won't fall.
Underneath the shady quilt,
Fruits spin tales, all lovingly built.

At dusk they gather, sharing jokes,
Running wild, those cheeky folks.
Sipping nectar, dreams take flight,
In the orchard's glow, we laugh through night!

Secrets in the Summer Breeze

In the breeze, secrets drift along,
Melodies weave through the fruit's song.
Bananas dance in yellow delight,
Flipping in circles, what a sight!

Crisp apples gossip in the shade,
About the berries and their parade.
Watermelons giggle with glee,
Every slice holds a sweet mystery.

Ticklish vines tickle toes aloud,
Fruits forming a playful crowd.
Whispers of sweetness fill the air,
Caught in laughter, a fruity affair.

Evenings glow with sunset's grace,
Fruity friends embrace the space.
In the summer's warmth, we tease,
Flavors dance upon the breeze!

Breezy Tales from the Orchard

In the orchard, fruits gather round,
Their giggles echo with a merry sound.
A fruit with a grin, a juicy delight,
Dance on the breeze, what a funny sight!

The apples tease, they bicker and shout,
'We're crunchier than you!' the pears knock about.
A round little berry, so plump and so sweet,
Claims it's the best; oh, what a treat!

With every plop, there's a new fruity jest,
A ripe little banana might just be the best.
They roll and they tumble, in colors so bright,
Their laughter, a melody, a pure, funny flight.

But the drippy old melon cries out with glee,
'You think you're the best? Just wait and see!'
With a splat and a splatter, he steals the show,
And the orchard erupts in a delighted glow!

Sipping the Summer's Splendor

A pitcher of fruit, oh what a delight,
Sipping and slurping from morning to night.
Each sip tells a tale, so funny and bright,
Of zesty adventures in the sun's warm light.

Citrus giggles while berries burst forth,
'We're the life of the party!' they share their worth.
The lemons make puns, oh, what a zany crew,
As they bounce in the glass with a cheerful hue.

Watermelons grumble, 'Too thick for the tub!'
But spice them with mint, and they join in the hub.
With bubbles and fizz, the laughter will rise,
As fruits splash and dance, oh, it's quite the prize.

So raise up your glasses, let's cheer and let's sing,
For every funny fruit a jester can bring.
In summer's bright sun, together we'll play,
With each silly sip, we'll laugh the day away!

Under the Shade of Sweetness

Beneath the broad leaves, where the cool breezes flow,
Fruits swap their stories, with a chuckle and glow.
A peach whispers secrets, a pear rolls its eyes,
While strawberries snicker at the clouds in the skies.

A fig cracks a joke about life on the vine,
While cherries chortle, sipping sweet brine.
The grapes form a circle, they're dancing in twos,
Spinning and twirling in colorful hues.

There's much fun to be had in this fruity parade,
With picnics and pranks in the fine, sunlit shade.
The mango trips over, what a clumsy blunder,
But the laughter erupts, louder than thunder!

So join in the frolic, let's savor the cheer,
Under bright banners we'll toast with good beer.
For in this warm orchard, joy's never in lack,
With every sweet moment, we'll never look back!

The Quiet Burst of Delight

In the stillness of evening, there's a hush in the air,
When fruits plot fun plans without any care.
Out pops a raspberry, with a silly little squeak,
'Oh, what a jester am I, cheeky and geek!'

The cantaloupe in the corner makes a bold move,
With a wink and a laugh, has the group on the groove.
'Let's make a parade!' shouts the old, wise lime,
And they chuckle in secret, oh, what a good time!

Each bite is a giggle, every nibble a jest,
As sweetness surrounds them, they feel truly blessed.
Like bubbles in soda, they fizz in delight,
Celebrating the moment, oh, what a silly sight!

So here's to the fruits and their whimsical ways,
Bursting with joy in the twilight's soft gaze.
For every small laugh, every burst of delight,
Brings forth the joy that glows in the night!

Nectar's Soft Confession

In the garden, giddy smiles,
Fruit in hiding, playing styles.
Gush of sweetness, bold delight,
Under sun, a juicy fight.

Sipping laughter, seeds do dance,
Every drip, a quirky chance.
With a giggle, colors burst,
Oh, the joy we cannot thirst!

Slice the joy, it's quite a thrill,
Taste the hope, enjoy the chill.
Call it whimsy, call it art,
What a way to lift the heart!

Summer's banquet steals the show,
With a wink, let laughter flow.
Cartwheels on the picnic ground,
Fruitful joy all around found!

The Hidden Heart of Harvest

Beneath the green, they start to hide,
Growing secrets, cheeky pride.
One plump buddy, quite a tease,
Winks at us with silly ease.

Round the corner, laughter spills,
Nature's jokes bring endless thrills.
Juicy giggles, sweet surprise,
Beneath the sun, the fun soon flies.

Rinds like armor, fit for jest,
Who knew that fruits could be so blessed?
Peeking out with cheeky charms,
Summer's bounty, spreading arms!

Harvest dances, all in tune,
Underneath the laughing moon.
In the field of funny hearts,
The joy of nature ever starts!

A Symphony of Summer's Core

The festival of colors bright,
A fruity stage, what a sight!
Ballet of flavors, round and bold,
Whispered stories, yet untold.

Slicing rhythms, nectar drops,
Playful giggles, never stops.
A chorus of joy fills the air,
With each bite, we shed a care.

Juicy melodies from the vine,
Tunes of laughter, oh so fine!
Twirling friends all gather near,
As we share, the fun is clear.

Symphony of sunlit cheer,
Sticky hands and happy peers.
Nature's humor on parade,
In this dance, we're unafraid!

Whispers of the Vine

Listen closely, laughter swells,
In the orchard, mischief dwells.
Round the paths, delightful pranks,
Fruits like chatter, sweet hijinks!

Underneath the leafy shade,
Silly games, let's not evade.
Friends and fruit in jolly cheer,
Every secret, we hold dear.

Tickle the ground, watch them roll,
Nature's laughter fills the whole.
Ripened jests, a harvest song,
In this moment, we belong.

Vines that twist with playful flair,
Whispers travel through the air.
Join the chorus, laugh and sway,
In the fields, we dance and play!

Sweet Lullabies of Green

In the patch where cucumbers roam,
Laughter dances, a giddy gnome.
With giggles that burst, like bubbles in air,
The fruit-chefs all whisper, 'What a funny affair!'

Round and round, they roll and they spin,
Roses tease daffodils, free to chime in.
A watermelon juggles, oh what a sight,
Slipping and sliding, my goodness, what a fright!

The peas play cards under leafy delight,
With radishes betting 'til the cool of night.
As crickets chuckle, the fruits share a grin,
In this hullabaloo, you can't help but join in!

From the sill of a window, the stories fly free,
Snapdragons giggle, oh what jubilee!
In this jovial patch, where none take a nap,
Sweet lullabies hum, filling all with a clap!

Slice of Sunset's Kiss

Under a sky brushed with rosy delight,
The cantaloupe smiles as day turns to night.
With each slice eager to share all the fun,
And watermelons waving, 'Let's eat, everyone!'

Peach and pear in a friendly embrace,
Telling tall tales about their sweet race.
The plums roll around, not a care to be seen,
Giggling and snorting, what a funny scene!

Berries on bushes are tasting the breeze,
Sipping the sunshine with such joyful ease.
A zesty lime joins the comedic charade,
Making us laugh at the puns it's made!

As lemon drops tumble in cheerful delight,
They spread all their sweetness, a glorious sight.
With slices of sunset, we can't help but cheer,
In a riot of flavors, we hold each dear!

Garden Serenade in Bloom

In a garden alive with whispers of cheer,
The fruits all gather, inviting us near.
A raspberry tickles a shy strawberry,
While the poppy joins in on the fruit-flavored spree!

Beneath the broad leaves, where adventures await,
The avocados gossip, 'We're feeling first-rate!'
Bananas swing gently from their leafy throne,
As cherries crack jokes that set the tone!

The zucchinis munch on fresh tales of delight,
While pumpkins recite punchlines, ever so bright.
Each flower a witness, each fruit a fan,
In this garden of giggles, let fun be the plan!

With petals and berries in vibrant array,
We dance through the patches, celebrating play.
This serenade whispers of joy and of bloom,
And laughter erupts in this colorful room!

The Taste of Sunlit Laughter

In fields of sunshine, where giggles sprout,
There's a feast of flavors, no doubt about.
With honeydew tales spun just for you,
And laughter that flutters like butterflies do!

The squash tells a story, oh what a tease,
As it shares its bright recipe with the breeze.
A cantaloupe chuckles, 'Come take a bite!'
While the corn joins in, tipping its hat just right!

Cheeky young lemons make puns on the fly,
As they squeeze out laughter that makes spirits fly.
Fruits play together in sun's warm embrace,
Creating a party, a delightful place!

With sweet-tasting joy, oh what a bright aftermath,
Every child giggles, joining the path.
For in every bite, there's sunlight to share,
And in every giggle, the world seems more fair!

Secrets Cradled in the Crop

In the patch, where secrets hide,
Laughter blooms on every side.
Round and green, a plump surprise,
Giggles pulse where sweetness lies.

Cucumbers blush and carrots grieve,
Witty whispers, none believe!
Strawberries grinning, oh what fun,
Jokes shared under the warm sun.

Pumpkins ponder what to wear,
While peas gossip without a care.
All the veggies have a say,
Their playful pranks brightening the day.

Even corn watches with a grin,
Cheering on the leafy kin.
So next time you find some cheer,
Remember the giggles grow near.

Reflection in the Juicy Abyss

In the pool of summer's glow,
Fruits discuss which way to go.
Pineapples wear their crowns with pride,
While oranges try to slide and ride.

Berries boast of their sweet tales,
While avocados spin on scales.
Radishes chatter, still underground,
Dreaming of the fun they found.

Lemons waltz with a zesty jig,
As lettuce laughs, coming alive big.
Splashes of juice, laughter juices,
In a carnival of fruity muses.

But beware the melon king's chuckle,
As he plans a juicy shuffle.
Dive into the sweet abyss,
Where fruity dreams do persist.

The Language of Ripeness

In the garden, ripe and round,
Chatter of colors can be found.
Peaches blush and pineapples wink,
In every fruit, a joke to think.

Grapes giggle with a tiny voice,
Making fermented choices rejoice.
A banana slips with silly grace,
While cherries flash a cheeky face.

Fruits of every shade and hue,
Chatting softly, just us two.
When summer calls, they break the rules,
For laughter's fruit is sunshine tools.

Lemon twists, a citric grin,
In this juicy world, we all win.
Let's savor each playful bite,
In ripeness, there's pure delight.

Summer's Hidden Conversation

In the field where shadows play,
Fruits are swapping tales today.
Pod of peas, a witty crew,
With whiny beans and laughter too.

Tomatoes roll with laughter's cut,
Telling tales of hungry rut.
Zucchini flexes, big and sly,
With dreams of being baked pie high.

Raspberries grinning, sweet and neat,
Share juicy secrets, none repeat.
Watermelons plot their speech,
In patches where they love to breach.

As summer wanes, the chatter flows,
With jokes and jests that no one knows.
So listen close when veggies meet,
For laughter grows in summer's heat.

Serenade of Sun Burst Bites

In the garden where fruit smiles,
Juicy tales beguile, and coax guilt-free trials.
With every slice, laughter erupts,
Sticky fingers dance, sweet nectar erupts.

Baskets brimmed with vibrant cheer,
Sunshine giggles, summer's here!
Lemonade laughs, a twist of lime,
Each sip, a tickle, a taste sublime.

Under the tree, we lounge and munch,
Sweet treats in laughter, oh what a bunch!
A fruity feast, it's merry and light,
In this banquet, all worries take flight.

Jesters of juice with a wink and a grin,
Infusing joy with every spin.
Whimsical bites, a festival spree,
In every crunch, we hear nature's glee.

Scented Pages of Epicurean Lore

Turns of the page unveil a dream,
Where every fruit bursts, ripe with steam.
Recipes rumble with playful tones,
An ode to delights, in hushed undertones.

Peachy prose and honeyed tales,
Giggles hidden in juicy trails.
Each platter swirls with giggly delight,
An open book, oh what a sight!

The ink flows brighter with every taste,
Mirthful servings, no time to waste.
A banquet of laughter in every line,
Scribbles of flavors, all wildly divine.

We flip through tales, a banquet grand,
With fruity metaphors, we take a stand.
In the kitchen, we sing and we twirl,
Serving up smiles in a fruity whirl.

The Art of Nature's Palette

Canvas brushed with green and gold,
Nature's humor, a joy to behold.
Slices of joy stack up in a bowl,
Each a bright whisper that tickles the soul.

Pops of color, a vibrant array,
Crisp little giggles, by the way.
Rainbow rendezvous in every bite,
With every crunch, the day's feeling bright.

Brushstrokes of flavor, tangy and sweet,
In a tableau where sunshine meets.
Artistic bites on a sunny spree,
Nature's own laughter, wild and free.

In culinary dance, we sway and cheer,
A masterpiece crafted, love is near.
Fruits parade, in joyous decree,
A flavorful canvas, come taste with me.

Summer Soliloquies of Flavor

Beneath the sun, each fruit does sing,
Merry melodies in each splash and fling.
Here comes the berry, with a wink and a tease,
Its juicy secrets put my heart at ease.

With each burst, a story threads,
A whimsical saga, where laughter spreads.
Flavored whispers of tang and sweet,
In summer's embrace, we dance to the beat.

Tropical dreams on this sunny stroll,
Each skewer of fruit fills the role.
Chasing the giggles, my taste buds swoon,
Sneaking in bites by the light of the moon.

In a bowl of sunshine, joy collides,
Flavorful antics that each one abides.
Let's toast to summer, let laughter prevail,
In this soliloquy, we revel and sail.

Summer's Sweetest Confessions

In the garden bright and bold,
Fruits of laughter, tales unfold.
Sticky fingers, juicy smiles,
Underneath the sun's warm styles.

Slicing whispers through the air,
Belly laughs without a care.
Each bite's a slippery jest,
Nature's jesters, truly blessed.

Teasing tongues with flavors sweet,
Dancing feet in joyful beat.
Underneath the azure sky,
Sweetest secrets, oh my, oh my!

Children giggle, shadows sway,
Tickled by the sun's ballet.
In this realm of juicy dreams,
Life is better than it seems.

The Language of Sun-Kissed Fruits

Silly smiles and tangled vines,
Fruitful puns in sweet designs.
Juicy gossip, laughter flies,
Nature's humor, no disguise.

Bananas giggle, berries tease,
Ripe with jokes that never freeze.
Peaches blush, they're cheeky too,
What a tasty, funny crew!

Citrus laughs in zesty tones,
Melodies from plump cone homes.
Whimsical with every bite,
Sunlit fun, a pure delight!

Watermelon's proud parade,
Giggles splash, no need for shade.
In this orchard, joy than flows,
Life's a fruitcake, goodness grows.

Whispering Fields of Green

Fields of green, where laughter plays,
Joyful whispers through the days.
Breezy jokes on petals sway,
Nature's humor on display.

Underneath the shady trees,
Silly voices ride the breeze.
Every leaf a comic tale,
In this patch, we'll never fail.

Bouncing beetles, funny bugs,
Ticklish bugs in playful hugs.
Roots that chuckle, branches sway,
Sun-kissed fruits in wild ballet.

In the field, we share our glee,
Each ripe nugget's jubilee.
Whispers grow beneath our feet,
Life is juicy, oh so sweet!

Ripe with Secrets of the Earth

Digging deep for jokes untold,
Roots of wonder, bright and bold.
In the ground, the giggles sprout,
Nature keeps us laughing out.

Harvest secrets, plump and round,
Earth's own punsters underground.
From the soil, the stories rise,
In the garden, laughter flies.

Every seed a joke in bloom,
Fruits of humor, sweet perfume.
When they ripen, we all cheer,
Bountiful bounty, never fear!

Underneath the sun so bright,
We find giggles in the light.
Ripe with joy, our hearts agree,
Life's a feast, come dance with me!

The Aroma of Joyful Abundance

In summer's heat they giggle loud,
A fruity burst, a joyful crowd.
Their round and shiny skins so bright,
Kick start the day, pure delight.

A picnic spread, they steal the scene,
With slices served, they're fit for queens.
Laughter blends with juicy drips,
As sticky fingers dance on lips.

The rinds become a children's game,
Inventing fun, they're never tame.
A cabin crew of buzzing bees,
Joining in sweet symphonies.

So pass the bowl, let's share the cheer,
These funny fruits keep smiles near.
They roll around without a care,
Joyful abundance everywhere!

Secrets Clinging to the Breeze

The garden murmurs, whispers low,
With secrets only we can know.
Among the greens, a raucous laugh,
Nature's prank in every half.

A breeze so light bears hints of fun,
As veggies dance beneath the sun.
The leaves are giggling, what a scene,
In shadows cast by sunlit green.

Each fruit a tale, a merry jest,
The juiciest plots, we're truly blessed.
They twirl and spin as if to tease,
Magic lingers on the breeze.

So come and sip the flavor's song,
Join the feast where we belong.
A slice of humor, joy, and zest,
In gardens, even smiles can rest!

Sweet Reflections in the Morning Dew

The dew drops glisten, a morning's wink,
With sweet reflections, don't you think?
A sticky joy, they drape like jewels,
Nature's grace, a dance for fools.

Each slice reveals a world of cheer,
The sunny flavors drawing near.
Laughter bubbles, in each delight,
As breakfast sparkles, oh, what a sight!

The bouncing seeds take flight and soar,
Chasing giggles, calling for more.
In every bite, a tale unfolds,
The funniest truths that life beholds.

So sip your tea, enjoy the view,
With sweet reflections, dreams come true.
The morning whispers bring us fun,
In every drop, adventures run!

The Untold Stories of Garden Delights

Beneath the sun, a tale unwinds,
With garden treasures, joy it finds.
A slice of laughter, vibrant cheer,
The secret stories whispered here.

Each fruit offers a wink, a tease,
With shades of humor in the breeze.
Giggles follow them as they roll,
Their playful charm takes quite a toll.

From tiny seeds to grand careers,
The garden's heart beats loud with cheers.
A feast of colors, scents collide,
In every corner, joy resides.

So gather round, let laughter flow,
With tales of garden delights aglow.
A symphony of tastes await,
In nature's club, we celebrate!

Juicy Secrets of Summer

In the sun, the fruits all gossip,
With giggles and snickers, they never stop!
Red cheeks blush as they bask in light,
Witty fruits dancing, a playful sight.

Lemon's sour, making lime pout,
While cherries prank, too loud to shout.
Watermelon winks, a joker's grin,
In the fruit bowl, chaos does begin!

Peaches stick close to the plumpest grapes,
Spinning tales of summer escape.
Bananas slip with laughter loud,
In this fruity world, they're all so proud!

Under the shade, they share a dream,
Tickled by the breeze, a playful team.
Secrets of summer, ripe and fun,
In the orchard, we're never done!

The Fruit's Silent Song

Sassy berries sway in the breeze,
Whispers floating through the leafy trees.
An avocado hums, deep and low,
While ripe figs giggle at the show.

Apples roll with a chuckle and spin,
Every fresh bloom knows where to begin.
Pineapples sport their crowns so proud,
Chanting secrets above the crowd.

A lively dance beneath the sun's glow,
Lemonade joins with the sweetest flow.
Quiet laughs echo, soft yet bright,
In every bite, pure delight!

From orchard to table, the joy is clear,
Nature's melody, oh so dear!
In every crunch and every slice,
Fruit's funny whispers, oh so nice!

Orchard Echoes at Dusk

Evening paints the sky in gold,
Fruits tell stories, some brave, some bold.
Pears share tales of summer's heat,
While vibrant berries tap their feet.

The plums plot mischief, a sly little crew,
Cantaloupes beam with a sunny view.
Ripe red cherries form a band,
Under twilight, all perfectly planned.

Grapes roll around, laughing with glee,
Debating the juiciest history.
With every breeze, they sway and glide,
Their fruity antics they never hide.

As dusk settles over the farm,
The orchard hums with fragrant charm.
The echoes of laughter linger long,
In this fruity world, we all belong!

Beneath the Rind: A Tale

Beneath their skins, secrets reside,
Fruits giggling softly, no need to hide.
Watermelon whispers of sweet summer nights,
While citrus zings with electric delights.

Underneath, the pulp has a tale,
Of silly adventures that never pale.
Kiwi's fuzzy hedges guard dreams so grand,
While cantaloupe lovers take a stand.

Bananas peel away the serious frown,
Throwing jokes at each other all around.
Strawberries blush, for laughter is sweet,
In the hidden world, they dance on their feet.

So gather 'round, let the fun unfold,
In the fruity kingdom, be brave and bold.
With every crunch, a story is spun,
In this juicy realm, we've all just begun!

www.ingramcontent.com/pod-product-compliance
Lightning Source LLC
Chambersburg PA
CBHW060143230426
43661CB00003B/553